I Can Make
REMARKABLE
ROBOTS

by Kristina A. Holzweiss
and Amy Barth

Rookie STAR™
Makerspace Projects

TABLE OF CONTENTS

ARE YOU A MAKER? 4

MAKING CAN HAPPEN ANYWHERE! 6

PROJECT 1
YOU CAN MAKE A DRAWBOT 7

PROJECT 2
YOU CAN MAKE A ROBOTIC HAND 13

PROJECT 3
YOU CAN MAKE A ROBOTIC ARM 19

DRAWBOT

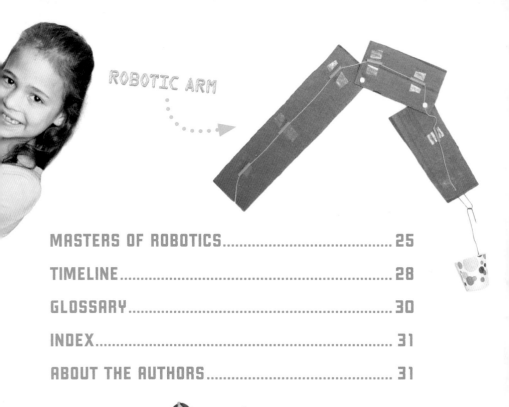

ROBOTIC ARM

MASTERS OF ROBOTICS.................................... 25

TIMELINE.. 28

GLOSSARY.. 30

INDEX.. 31

ABOUT THE AUTHORS.. 31

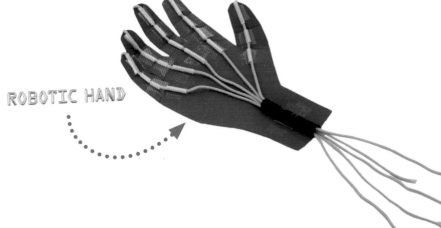

ROBOTIC HAND

ARE YOU A MAKER?

Makers are inventors, artists, and builders. In this book, you will learn how to make three remarkable robots: a drawbot, a robotic hand, and a robotic arm.

These projects look very different from each other. But they have something in common—they are all **robotic**.

Anyone can be a maker. You don't need fancy tools. You don't need to be a computer whiz. Are you creative and up for an adventure? Then you've got what it takes. Let's get started!

DRAWBOT

ROBOTIC ARM

ROBOTIC HAND

5

MAKING CAN HAPPEN ANYWHERE!

You don't need a workshop to be a maker. You can make things in a classroom or on your kitchen floor. Project materials can be found around the house or at a craft shop.

You will need an adult's help with some steps. Like all inventors, you will try out your robots. Then you will change your designs to make them even better.

YOU CAN MAKE A DRAWBOT

A drawbot is a simple robot that buzzes along on a piece of paper. As it moves, it scribbles colorful designs. You can decorate your drawbot any way you like. Give it a personality! What doodles will your drawbot make?

HOW A DRAWBOT WORKS

BODY
This is the outside of your robot.

MOTOR
There is an electric toothbrush inside your drawbot. When the toothbrush vibrates, the drawbot moves.

LEGS
Three markers are the robot's three legs. The legs keep the drawbot from toppling over.

DOODLES
As the drawbot moves, the markers draw on the paper.

Scientists know that even objects that look like they are standing still are really moving on the inside. That is because the smallest part of anything is an **atom**. And atoms are constantly in motion.

DISCOVER MORE ABOUT

VIBRATION

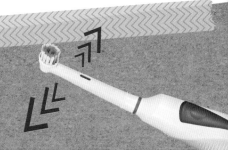

Vibration is when something moves rapidly back and forth or up and down. Other words for vibrate are shake, tremble, and rattle.

Inside your drawbot, the electric toothbrush vibrates when it is switched on. These vibrations shake the drawbot, making it move along the paper.

YOU WILL NEED

- ☐ Battery
- ☐ Battery-powered toothbrush
- ☐ Scissors or knife
- ☐ Pool noodle
- ☐ Duct tape
- ☐ Three thin markers (Choose your favorite colors!)
- ☐ White school glue
- ☐ Googly eyes, pipe cleaners, feathers, pom-poms, yarn, etc.
- ☐ Plain white paper

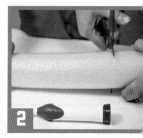

1 Insert the battery into the toothbrush.

2 Ask an adult for help with the scissors or knife. Cut the pool noodle to the length of the toothbrush.

3

ush the toothbrush
rough the center
f the noodle. Make
ure the brush part
  at the top.

4

Tape the markers to
the bottom of the
noodle. They should
extend about
3 inches past the
end of the noodle.

5

Decorate your
drawbot. Be as
creative as possible!

MAKE IT MOVE

Place the piece of paper on a flat
surface. Remove the caps from the
markers. Turn on the toothbrush.
Place the drawbot on the paper,
and let go!

CHANGE IT

····▶ Use crayons or pencils instead of markers. How do the different writing tools change your drawbot's doodles? Are the drawings lighter or brighter?

····▶ Does changing to crayons or pencils change the sizes and shapes of your doodles?

····▶ Does changing to crayons or pencils change how smoothly your drawbot moves?

····▶ Make one marker longer than the others. What happens?

TEST IT

Does your drawbot move across the paper? What types of designs does it draw as it travels?

PROJECT 2

YOU CAN MAKE A ROBOTIC HAND

We use our hands to eat, get dressed, write, play sports, and much more! Wouldn't it be great to have an extra hand to help out? Robotic hands can grab and hold things, like a fork or a pencil. You can make a robotic hand!

13

HOW HANDS WORK

Your hand is made up of different parts that work together so you can do things like hold a fork, type on a computer, and give a high five.

BONES
A hand is made up of 27 bones. Bones give a hand its shape.

JOINTS
Joints are where two bones connect. This allows body parts to bend.

TENDONS
Tendons connect muscle to bone.

MUSCLES
Muscles help power your hand so you can wiggle your fingers and bend your wrist.

THUMB
The thumb is what makes us able to grasp and hold onto things.

Wiggle your fingers. See how your thumb moves differently than your other fingers? That is because humans have opposable thumbs. Your thumb can bend across the other fingers on your hand. This gives people the ability to grasp things, pick up small objects, and eat with one hand.

DISCOVER MORE ABOUT

OPPOSABLE THUMBS

Humans are not the only ones with opposable thumbs. All great apes like chimps, gorillas, and orangutans have them, too! Opposable thumbs help apes swing from tree branches and peel fruit. They help people use tools, throw baseballs, grasp pencils, and much more. Can you think of anything else?

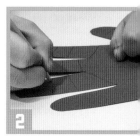

YOU WILL NEED

- ☐ Pencil
- ☐ Thin cardboard or card stock
- ☐ Scissors
- ☐ Three narrow, straight plastic drinking straws
- ☐ Clear tape
- ☐ Wide, straight plastic drinking straw
- ☐ Yarn or string, cut into five equal pieces 1½-2 feet long

1 Trace an adult's hand and wrist onto the cardboard or card stock. Make sure the fingers are spread open. Cut out the hand and wrist.

2 Mark three joints on each finger except for the thumb. Mark two joints on the thumb. Draw a line across each joint. Fold the fingers on these lines.

MAKE IT MOVE

Place your robotic hand on a flat surface with the straw side facing up. Keep it in place by holding down the wrist. Use your free hand to pull the strings. This creates **tension**, and curls the robot's fingers inward. Try to make the robotic hand count on its fingers from one to five.

3

ut four pieces of
arrow straw for
ch finger. The
eces should match
e length of each
nger segment.
pe one piece onto
ch segment, and
e right below,
the palm. Make
re you don't cover
e joints. Cut three
eces of narrow
raw for the
umb. Repeat
e placement.

4

Cut the wide plastic
straw in half. Tape
one piece to the
wrist of the hand.

5

Pass pieces of yarn
through the wrist
straw and then
through each
finger straw.

6

Fold the end of
each piece of yarn
over the tips of the
fingers. Tape them
in place.

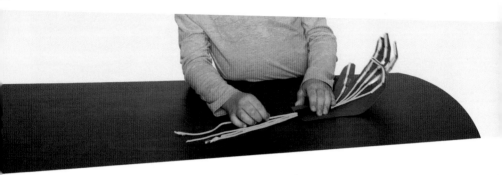

TEST IT

Place an apple in the palm of the robotic hand and pull on the strings. Do the fingers fully grasp the apple?

CHANGE IT

····▶ Try grasping something smaller with the robotic hand—like a ping-pong ball or a cotton ball.

····▶ Tape one long piece of straw to each finger instead of three small straw pieces. The hand no longer has joints. How does that change the robot's ability to grasp?

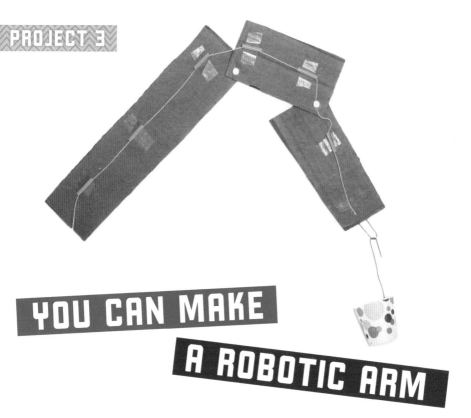

YOU CAN MAKE

A ROBOTIC ARM

Robotic arms are much stronger than human arms. They can help people lift heavy objects. Robotic arms are used in space. The *Mars Rover*, a machine that explores the planet Mars, has a robotic arm. Its arm can scoop up soil. You can make a robotic arm!

HOW A ROBOTIC ARM WORKS

BONE

The cardboard strips are the arm bones.

JOINT

The brass fasteners are the arm's joints. They allow the arm to bend.

MUSCLE

The string is the arm muscle. That powers the arm to help it move.

TENDON

The straws are tendons. They connect bones (cardboard) to muscle (string).

Place a fairly light object, like a tennis ball or an apple, on a table. Now grab the object and pick it up. Did you feel your fingers, hand, and arm muscles become tense? That is what makes you able to pick up the object. Now pick up something heavier. Do your muscles need to be more or less tense to pick up a heavier object?

DISCOVER MORE ABOUT
TENSION

Tension is when something is stretched tight. To hold on to an object, muscles **contract**. This creates muscle tension. Your robotic arm uses tension to move. For it to work, the strings must be tense. If they are loose, the arm cannot lift things.

INSTRUCTIONS

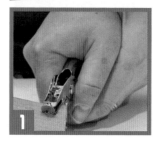

1

Ask an adult for help using the hole punch. Make a hole in one corner of each cardboard strip. Cut the straw into six 1-inch pieces.

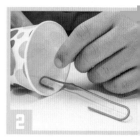

2

Unbend a paper clip to form a hook. Tape it to the inside of the cup to make a basket.

YOU WILL NEED

- ☐ Hole punch
- ☐ Three strips of corrugated cardboard:
  2 x 8 inches,
  2 x 6 inches,
  2 x 4 inches
- ☐ Scissors
- ☐ Ruler
- ☐ Plastic drinking straw, cut into six 1-inch pieces
- ☐ Two large paper clips
- ☐ Clear tape
- ☐ Paper cup
- ☐ Two 1-inch medium brass fasteners
- ☐ String, like fishing line (29 inches)

3

se the fasteners to onnect the small trip of cardboard o the long and nedium strips. o not make them oo tight.

MAKE IT MOVE

'ull the string to nake the arm end. Put the aper cup on a able. Hook the aper clip finger nto the cup. Can ou pull the string n the arm to lift he cup?

4

Lay three straw pieces lengthwise down the middle of the long strip. Lay two pieces down the middle of the small strip. Lay one straw piece on the medium strip.

5

Tape the straws in place. Starting at the end of the long strip, thread the string through the straw pieces. Tape the end of the string down on the medium strip, or hand.

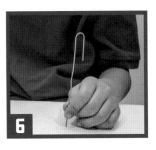

6

Unbend a paper clip to form a hook. This is a finger for your robotic arm.

7

Poke the straight end of the paperclip into the end of the cardboard hand.

23

TEST IT

What other objects can the arm lift? Try lifting something light, like a rubber band, and something heavier, like a doughnut!

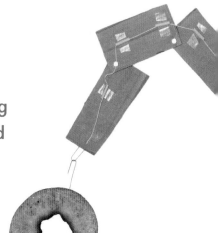

CHANGE IT

····► Replace the hook with a small, strong magnet. What kinds of things can you pick up with the robotic arm?

····► Attach a spoon to the robot arm. Can you pick up a fruity cereal loop and hand it to a friend?

····► Add more paper clip fingers to the hand. Can the robotic arm pick up something heavier now?

MASTERS

OF ROBOTICS

JACQUES DE VAUCANSON

Jacques de Vaucanson was a French inventor who lived during the 1700s. He built some of the earliest robots. One was a mechanical duck that quacked and flapped its wings. The mechanical duck had hundreds of moving parts!

KAREL CAPEK

Karel Capek was a writer from Czechoslovakia. He invented the word "robot." Capek used the word "robot" in his play *Rossum's Universal Robots*, which was performed in 1921. In the play, a scientist discovers how to create human-like machines.

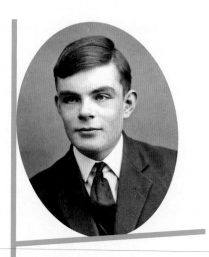

GEORGE DEVOL
JOE ENGELBERGER

ALAN TURING

Alan Turing was an English computer scientist. In 1950, he invented the "Turing Test," which determines whether machines can think like people do. Scientists are working on building smart robots that pass the test.

George Devol and **Joe Engelberger** were American inventors. They worked together to invent a robotic arm. The arm could grasp and lift objects. In the 1960s, they formed the world's first robot company, called Unimation.

ISAAC ASIMOV

Isaac Asimov was an American writer and biologist. In the 1950s, he began writing short stories and books about robots. One collection of stories is called *I, Robot.* His writing inspired future robot inventors.

TIMELINE:

FAMOUS ROBOTS

Check out this timeline about some of the coolest robots ever made.

1927
The first robot appears in a movie called *Metropolis.*

1939
Elektro, a robot that can walk and talk, is exhibited at the World's Fair in New York.

1966
Shakey is the first robot that can both move and act intelligently.

1977
The movie *Star Wars* debuts and makes stars of droids R2-D2 and C-3PO.

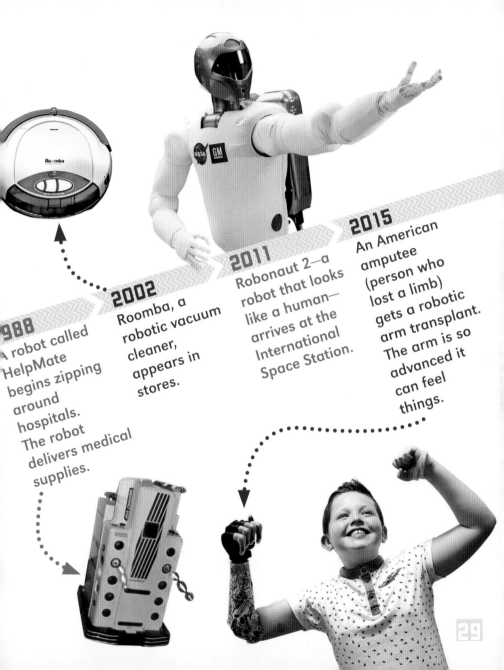

1988
A robot called HelpMate begins zipping around hospitals. The robot delivers medical supplies.

2002
Roomba, a robotic vacuum cleaner, appears in stores.

2011
Robonaut 2—a robot that looks like a human—arrives at the International Space Station.

2015
An American amputee (person who lost a limb) gets a robotic arm transplant. The arm is so advanced it can feel things.

Atom *(at-uhm)*

The tiniest part of an element that has all the properties of that element.

Contract *(kuhn-trakt)*

To shorten (as in a muscle) in order to cause a part of the body to move.

Robotic *(roh-bah-tic)*

Related to machines that are programmed to perform complex human tasks.

Tension *(ten-shuhn)*

The stiffness or tightness of something such as a rope or wire.

drawbot...................... 4, 7–12

opposable thumbs 15

robotic arm 4, 19–24

robotic hand 4, 13–18

vibration 9

ABOUT THE AUTHORS

Kristina A. Holzweiss was selected by School Library Journal as the School Librarian of the Year in 2015. She is the Founder of SLIME—Students of Long Island Maker Expo and the President of Long Island LEADS, a nonprofit organization to promote STEAM education and the maker movement. In her free time, Kristina enjoys making memories with her husband, Mike, and their three children, Tyler, Riley, and Lexy.

Scholastic Library Publishing wants to especially thank Kristina A. Holzweiss, Bay Shore Middle School, and all the kids who worked as models in these books for their time and generosity.

Amy Barth is a writer and editor specializing in science content for kids in elementary through high school. She writes about robots, penguins, volcanoes, and beyond! She lives in Los Angeles, California.

Library of Congress Cataloging-in-Publication Data

Names: Holzweiss, Kristina A., author. | Barth, Amy, 1984– author.
Title: I Can Make Remarkable Robots/by Kristina A. Holzweiss and Amy Barth.
Description: New York, NY: Children's Press, an imprint of Scholastic Inc., 2018.
| Series: Rookie star. Makerspace projects | Includes index.
Identifiers: LCCN 2017005031| ISBN 9780531234105 (library binding) |
ISBN 9780531238790 (pbk.)
Subjects: LCSH: Robotics—Juvenile literature. | Robots—Juvenile literature.
Classification: LCC TJ211.2 .H495 2018 | DDC 629.8/92—dc23
LC record available at https://lccn.loc.gov/2017005031

Design: Judith Christ-Lafond & Anna Tunick Tabachnik
Text: Kristina A. Holzweiss & Amy Barth
© 2018 Scholastic Inc.

All rights reserved. Published in 2018 by Children's Press, an imprint of Scholastic Inc.
Printed in China 62
SCHOLASTIC, CHILDREN'S PRESS and associated logos are trademarks and/or
registered trademarks of Scholastic Inc., 557 Broadway, New York, NY 10012.

1 2 3 4 5 6 7 8 9 10 R 27 26 25 24 23 22 21 20 19 18

Photos ©: 6 scissors: fotomy/iStockphoto; 6 tape: Carolyn Franks/Dreamstime; 6
glue gun: Nilsz/Dreamstime; 6 markers: Floortje/Getty Images; 6 straws and throughout: Olga Dubravina/Shutterstock; 6 marble: David
Arky/Getty Images; 6 CD: Roman Sigaev/Shutterstock; 6 bottle cap: Mrs_ya/Shutterstock; 6 pencil: antomanio/iStockphoto; 9 toothbrush:
StockPhotosArt/iStockphoto; 9 background and throughout: Hughstoneian/Dreamstime; 10 left and throughout: somchaij/Shutterstock;
14: Andy Crawford/Getty Images; 15: Daniela White Images/Getty Images; 18 bottom left: Astrug/Dreamstime; 21 center: Nagy-bagoly
Ilona/Dreamstime; 24 left: mayakova/iStockphoto; 24 right: colevineyard/iStockphoto; 25 left: ART Collection/Alamy Images; 25 center
left: Bettmann/Getty Images; 25 center right: Popperfoto/Getty Images; 25 right: Mary Evans Picture Library Ltd/age fotostock; 26 left:
Fine Art Images/Heritage Images/Getty Images; 26 right: From the Collections of The Henry Ford (THF222307); 27 top: Mario Suriani/AP
Images; 27 bottom: Album/Newscom; 28 left: Owen Murray/Alamy Images; 28 center left: Bettmann/Getty Images; 28 center right: SRI
International/Wikimedia; 28 right: United Archives GmbH/Alamy Images; 29 bottom left: Peter Menzel/Science Source; 29 top left: Doug-
las McFadd/Getty Images; 29 top right: NASA/Sipa USA/Newscom; 29 bottom right: Mark Runnacles/Getty Images; 30 top: chromatos/
iStockphoto; 30 bottom: Nagy-bagoly Ilona/Dreamstime; 30 center bottom: Mark Runnacles/Getty Images.

All instructional images by Jennifer A. Uihlein.
All other images by Bianca Alexis Photography.